I'm Thankful
For So Many Things

P.K. Hallinan

Ideals Publishing Corp.
Nashville, Tennessee

Copyright © MCMLXXXVI by Ideals Publishing Corp.
All rights reserved. Printed and bound in U.S.A.
Published simultaneously in Canada.

ISBN 0-8249-8158-8

I'm thankful each day
for the blessings I see
and for all of the gifts
that are given to me.

And counting the stars
at the edge of the sea,

I can't help but feel
they were put there for me.

I'm thankful for summers
and warm golden days...

I'm thankful for autumns
of orange pumpkin haze.

I'm thankful for meadows
and bright colored flowers...

I'm thankful for raindrops
and soft summer showers.

Each sunset is special...

each sunrise is new.

Each breeze in the trees
is a promise come true.

Each evening's a wonder
where beauty abounds.

Each morning's a harvest
of new sights and sounds.

And it's nice just to know
that beneath winter snow,
the blossoms of spring
are beginning to grow.

I'm thankful for friends
who sit by my side

and make me feel better
when I'm troubled inside.

And I'm thankful for friends
who come over to play

when there's nothing to do
on a wet rainy day.

Friends are just perfect for all kinds of things,

like walking...

or talking...

or swinging on
swings!

And for watching TV,
friends are the best

for cheering cartoons with,
and booing the rest.

And then late at night
friends are just right

for telling ghost stories
when you've turned off the light.

Yes, I'm thankful for friends
to hop, skip, or run with...

for playing some catch...

or just having fun with.

We can sing, we can shout
till our tonsils wear out,

'cause that's what having
a friend's all about!

I'm thankful for listeners
who listen with care

when I've got a big secret
I just have to share.

I'm thankful for buddies
who come to my aid

when they think I need help,
and I might be afraid.

I'm thankful for partners
who stand back to back
to protect me from bullies
or an injun attack.

And I'm thankful for friends
who just want to play
all of the games
we can play in one day!

We have our own hideouts
in dark, secret places
and spend the whole day
making very strange faces.

We can laugh...

we can cry...

we can watch cars go by...

we can have a great time
and not even try!

Yes, I'm thankful for friends,
for laughing and sharing...

I'm thankful for family,
for loving and caring.

I'm thankful for all the kindness I see...

I'm thankful for peace
and for pure harmony.

My body's a present
of perfect design...

my mind is a power
as endless as time.

And if ever I worry
that trouble is near,
I always remember
there is nothing to fear...

for each hour is laden
with infinite love...

each second brings comfort
and joy from above.

And I guess in the end
the best thing to say
is I'm thankful for living...

I'm thankful each day!